it's.

/ɪts/

pronoun + verb

just the next one, the new,

a volume two of two minute poems,

following era, the volume one,

written daily, almost, and all on @threads.

similar

they're, them's, he's, she's.

Haider Bahrani

to
mum
thank you

Contents

volume 2 of poems originally written on micro blogging site @threads each a little bit of the day's story and presented in reverse chronology

each was written and these were my rules ad hoc and in less than a minute or two

there is some light touch editing mostly in the first five minutes and a little bit as i put them together here for you

as you can tell i've left out the punctuation mostly

that i will leave up to you

the first line of nearly all is the title too

pinned thread

when i start
a bit of verse on here
i have no idea
what i will write next
nor the context
nor when
i end

this is at the start of each volume

it's
headline news
apples are
apparently
now blue
well surely
that's not true?
i have seen them
they are mostly
green
red
slightly yellow
maybe
but certainly
not
well
not in my view!
yet there it was
in big bold letters
i'm sure
there was a story
and i'm in a hurry
to go
post my opinion
so maybe you
can read it
for me

can i be bothered?
my past efforts have left a trail
an inventory of sorts
i was once the monarch of discourse
now with
my energy depleted
my only fuel is remorse
i have no mood
to stay this course
p.s. this is
a work of fiction
i am playing a part
this is not autobiographical art
but did i feel
every verse
as i was emersed
in my craft?
there may be mediocrity
in my ability
but i enjoy
every scribble
yes i sometimes use a pen
and every draft

prompted by:@caitltalks

"Caiti's Writing Prompts
Write about apathy
Include the words: trail, inventory, and
monarch"

i'm not sure
i have to choose
it's all last minute
and i'm panicking a bit
it's great
i haven't had to do
the donkey work
for several
weeks or days
and the samples
are narrowed down to two
the choice seems simple
you say
a kind of red
or the same
but a little less blue
but suddenly
i have to
make a decision
and you leave
in 5 minutes
to go and get them
a choice
not so frivolous
as it might seem
for i have
to live with it
yet this is what
us humans do
it's last minute
ok i can pretend
because you know
what happens
in the end
i like the red one
and you

will smile and go
and get the one
with a little less
blue

just a thought
if we all had one
about everything
in which we
become caught
would it be better than
if we more often
thought naught?

where was i?
oh hold on
as i was saying
and i can't lie
that's just it
i can't
it would be
forever playing
on my mind
the sweat
i'd be a mess
of anxiousness
i could probably
keep a secret
but every time
i lie
i would just
a little bit
die inside

and

it seems
i use it a lot
even though
many might say
i perhaps
should not
but
and i've often
tried not
i read through
and it flows
when other words
do not
so i decide
so what?
and not just that
another word
i've noticed
i used a lot
is not

madness

you could say
else why
would it be
that way?
as they show
zero remorse
they ate the sausages
yet left the beans
red ones
not the green
though i would
have had them too
ok maybe
it lacks the toast
and fried eggs
but still
for me
this is
a wonky pill
they didn't even
have them
with brown sauce!

you call it
an egg plant
i call it aubergine
you like it fried
i mushed up
with crushed sesame
and when they use it
in an emoji
neither
is what they mean
not a gram or an ounce
of either
makes that much sense
to me

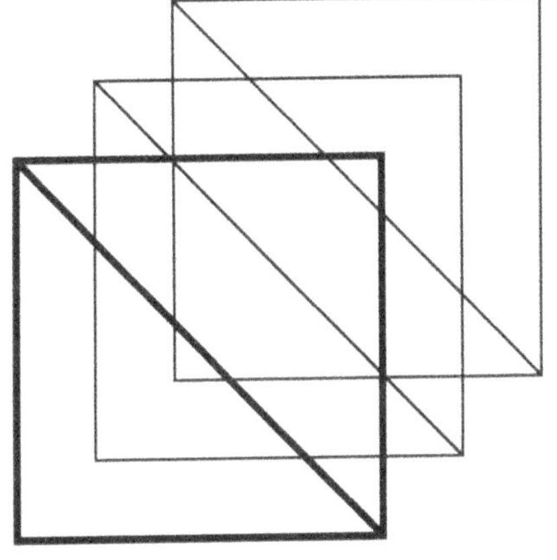

i tell you all
we're away
and having
so much fun
you now know
my birthday
my mother's
maiden name
and those
of my children
i hope
you've seen
and liked
all my pictures
and you know
how great i am
i tell you all
did i say?
we're away
and we'll be
a while
so you
now know
and so does
everyone!

a show

for some
the pretence
that's all it is
but as i am sure
you know
it makes sense
it's proximity
that makes us glow
a phone call
an email
a letter
it's all good and well
if you can't do
anything better
but to be there
not in anyone's hair
and even if
you are sometimes
it's almost always
worse
when you're not
there

music
keeps me here
takes me back
sometimes
to places
i was never at
yet i remember!
how odd is that?
music
carries me
to wherever
i ever
want to be at

phew
that was
quite a thing
i wasn't sure
if we'd manage
not till the end
it was challenging
and quite enough
even at the beginning
but the unexpected
things
that happened
during
sure brought on
the adrenaline
seems pointless
all that planning
excepting
the plans we had
for panicking

i can't decide
do i speak out
or do i hide?
sometimes
it's easier
just to let it slide
for you can't convince
a masher
that potatoes
are better
roasted
or fried

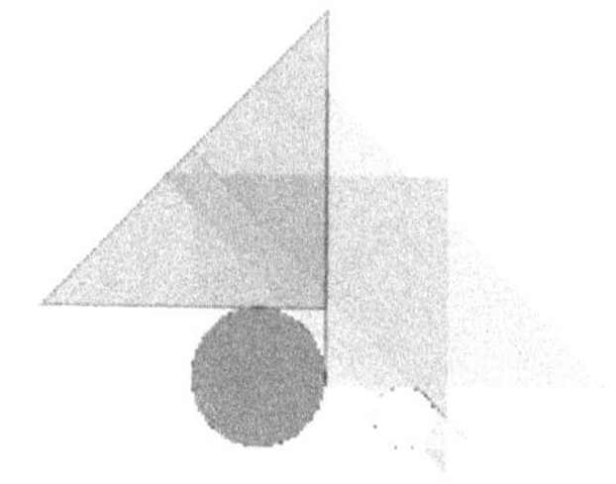

the bar

the bar
we go
to the bar
then a party
the bar
the bar
we go to
the bar
we live
we work
to go
to the bar
then
we hit
we hit
we hit
the bar
we hit
a bar
it's a mess
a mess
a mess

i must confess

what we do
what we do
we never rest
we never rest
we need a rest
lest we
arrest

yes today
is all
that matters
now
tomorrow
is important
and indeed
yes
plan
then if it comes
it will be
just as such
but with
so much
misfortune
and fate
going on
who knows
if and when
our tomorrow
will come?

more

it's a constant
want
a craving
the root of all
and the route
to a fall
but for desire
it might not be at all
be it for love
for lust
to just do
help
and be there
more

it's funny
this thing
about
the bunny
and the eggs
it's a good story
but
and this could just be
silly me
it seems
it has
no legs!

the bigger picture
i see how it is
important to some
an excuse
to more than one
idle in thought
for all their dreaming
of a better tomorrow
but at what cost?
when so much is
and many are
today lost
to not their cause
nor even a promised harvest
to feed their clear
and present
hunger
who will pleasure
in this utopian
lust
i wonder?

this is big

it's definitely news
well it seems to be
normally
i wouldn't express
any view
in fact it would
pass me by
and really
not make much
of an impression
but my daughter
is on a mission
to tell everyone
about
her new shoes

traffic
that's it
ching
ching
ching
i'll say
whatever
you want me to
ping
ping
ping

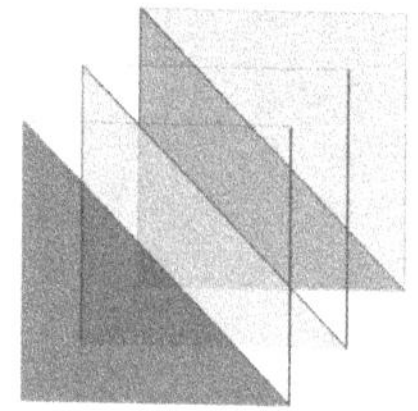

ah the stress
i must confess
i am not sure
i can maintain
my own decorum
my head
my stomach
my legs
my lungs
all those
that contort
hyper
and wobble
must form a forum
as to ascertain
why
just the idea
of eating
that thing
that promise
of a hay fever cure
feels like being
under duress?

cold

logic
some call it
rational thought
with it
we can
it is said
justify anything
and much of that
because of it
is bought
for logic might say
don't love
or grow old
hence the price
seems less
for warmth
and feeling
yet i would give
more for that
than just about
anything

wait
it's what we
mostly do
this isn't news
the idea
is definitely not
new
but a bit like
the universe
it's not called hydrogen
and we are not called
breathing
and a car
parking
life is called living
not waiting

i breathe

i walk
probably talk
i think
i think
i weave
with one thought
while another one
ponders
and others
draw links
between
my many wonders
things
make sense
then not
then i untie
the knots
to find it all
sort of
comes together
in the end
but there is no end
and that's the wonder
as i breathe
and i walk
it's often nice too
to talk

then it stops
just like that
with no word
or suggestion
of intention
it was something
a pleasure
a comfort
or just a regular
pleasant distraction
tomorrow
will be forever different
though much of it
much the same
and new plants will grow
whence they left
to give cause
to those who remain

where was i?
i was here
just now
i had an idea
but then
as i looked at you
my most companion
a ping
on another screen
made me lean
caught my thought
and ate it up
so when i looked back up
at you
my forever view
i had to think
of something new

i'm on the phone
he said
oh sorry but
she said
is it urgent
he said
no
she said
i'm on the phone sorry
he said
it's just i've spoken to and
she carried on
i'm on the phone
he said
you annoyed?
she asked
i'm on the phone
he harked
shall i come back in a bit?
she asked again
i'm on the phone
he sighed
you could have just said
she replied

if i bask in glory
on a story
with no real his
or herstory
then i suppose
i'm a fake
an emperor
caught in the shoals
with no clothes
a self gratifying
instance indeed
but no better
than the growth
of a weed
in the perfect turf
a temporary pick up
for my self worth
a narcotic addiction
an unfortunate
need

tonight
we go to sleep
then wake
we hope
and we write
the same song
and we sing along
we sing along
love song
after love song
as we pretend
that nothing
is ever wrong
well not more than
the odd
broken heart
and the anguish
of being apart
from those
we may even
have not yet met
to whom
we write
we write
another
love song

yes i agree
most definitely
it's time to be rid
of this outdated structure
where a club is exclusive
to one gender
with their special codes
and in jokes
come on mums
it's time
to let the dads
into the year group
chat group
nights out
and
chit chat

today
not so ordinary
yet like
my every day
we bumped
into one another
you were going this way
i with my mother the other
it was a smile
and good morning
yet from before
we had yet met
nor do we know
each other
and we carried on
feeling less invisible
less ignored
hopefully then too
the day
fractionally
better

oh!
was it?
i didn't realise
and really
didn't think
not much
of it
well it's passed
not a concern
nor do i need to atone
but if i'd known
they were your sweets
maybe
i would have
asked

morning
has broken
i'll try to fix it
and if i do
not that i crave it
will something
more divine
get the credit?

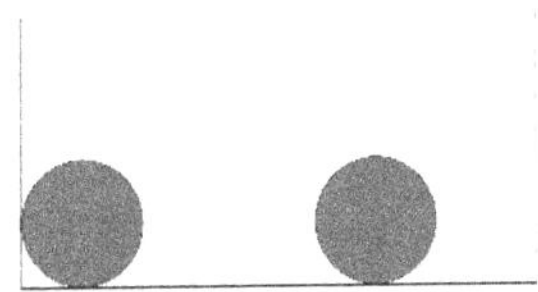

somewhere
in the universe
a star again
has faded
it's light
for a brief
moment
in time
shone
brightly
most didn't notice
but for something
or someone
and
like it
and all
we are not here
for very long
so today
and tomorrow
if it comes
for the sake
of your soul
keeping it whole
don't let anyone else
write your song

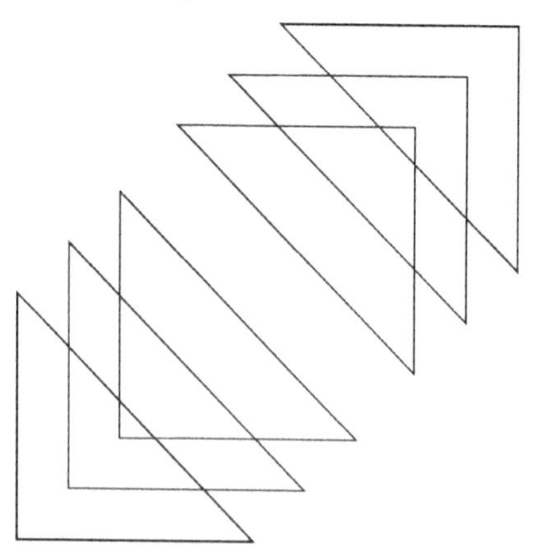

43

it happens
it happens
it happens
then not
we reminisce
when it stops

preaching
it's a thing
too often
it comes
without
listening
we would
mind less
if it was beseech
or implore
no moral high ground
and less of a bore
at least then
there's a chance
to let each other's
thoughts
share a floor
and a dance
preaching
on the other hand
can seem like
a more forced
romance

i confess
i have no idea
what it is
that keeps
everything tidy
despite the mess
but yes
and i am sure
many are with me here
the moment
it's tidied
we are helpless
the order of the mind
is not in straight lines
so why would it be
in how we prepare our lair
or how we dress?

a relief
to find the day
has so far
been ok
my toast not burnt
my coffee not spilled
and the kids
up on time
all their morning tasks
fulfilled
so a moment
of calm
'see if i can
keep dry palms
for the next
anticipated
event

the best
in practical fact
that we can do
to help each other
through
the days
when we
jump through
the same hoops
walk on the same
fiery paths
simply to act
to make it
more cheery
for each of us to do
for indeed good company
passes us more
quickly through
most difficult moments
and days
with a little less
anguish
and sometimes
turn times
unexpectedly
into something
to cherish

no

it's not true
i woke up this morning
and another year
fell to one side
the number
i write
when i fill in certain forms
grew
how can it be?
i was just
the other day
picking up my satchel
and going to school
but the century was different
and the music
groovy and cool

it was
looking like
a nothing day
finally
i can
just do things
where no one
other than me
has a say
well that was a ruse
a mirage
a cloud in my view
it wasn't long
before i was rushing
to put on my shoes
to fix something wrong
or do what someone else
couldn't or wouldn't do
it still felt like nothing done
my time stolen
my seams undone
a nothing day
indeed but
not the one
i need

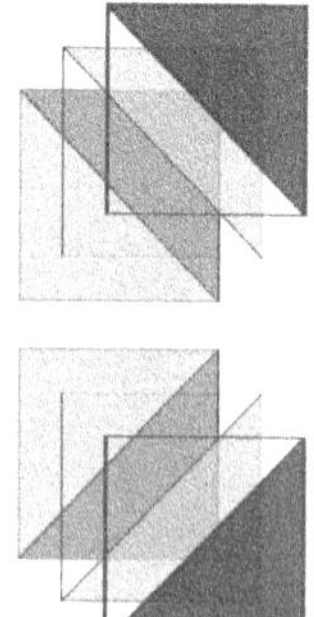

older

and wiser
wise enough
to know
life is better
and more fun
to be bolder
and do things
less wise
that to some
deemed
wrong

fine

grit your teeth
pretend
you don't mind
or just
it's not
really a good time
so a word we use
to cover up
to carry on
or it's simply
the ordinary
everything's ok
but nothing
really new
truth

me
the centre
of my attention
i
if there is one thing
that makes me
nervous
uncomfortable
sometimes cry
i
could be
the only one
in the room
with a microphone
in my face
on a boom
a guitar on my lap
a pen and paper
me
the centre of my attention
is no fun caper
can you imagine
more than one
judging
thinking
even i
imagine
knowing
though
i am too hoping
you reading this
gives me that feeling
i'm sinking

go ahead
do something
act on a whim
it's hard
being a cog
in a machine
to get out
and just be
yes the well oiled
refined unit
that you have read
you should be
let's you have breakfast
at 7.45
be thrice weekly
at the gym
and tea at 3.15
but then
what does it
all mean?

silence

what a pleasure
it came
heaven sent
then it went
what a wonderful
few ticks
less than a minute
if only
the noise
and its tricks
left with it

i think
i've probably
written this
once or twice before
but i am no one
no one more
than anyone
if i claim to be
anything
that is beyond
the wilder imagination
then that
is not me
i have exaggerated
a little perhaps
on a night out
when the excitement
has made my lips lapse
into delusion
embellishment
and yes
more than that little
exaggeration
so please
we all have
a story to tell
some tell it so well
it's no more than a coin
in the wishing well

clarity is all

we try
in different ways
each of us
to convey
our minds
our thoughts
or just
to make
a presentation
of the facts
though sometimes
as we act
with good intention
we get in a jumble
we over mention
over present
or keep our words
too few
because
we can't all be so clear
so sure
so confident
so yes
clarity
is all
but it's hard
to be clear
to everyone's ear

all
we had to do
was wait
they would lay
another bait
when even
breathing
becomes
a competition
they won't be happy
till you're late

i dare not
certainly not
in haste
just in case
i don't get
what i hope
or expect
if it goes well
which
as i dwell
i expect
not

the centre

of attention
it's a cause
for some
and
the effort
to attain it
sees no pause
the centre
on reflection
to be the
one and only
is very
lonely

we
in our many
doctrine
guised
as philosophy
ideology
and often
religion
seek to protect
the innocent
but your innocent
is not necessarily mine
if i adopt their thoughts
and not yours
then neither
am i

love it

well
not really
but it's
made them
so happy
so
i can't say
what i really
mean
that
in context
would be
quite mean
and they
have to live with it
not me
and they
love it
at least
that's what
both of them
say when
in each others'
company

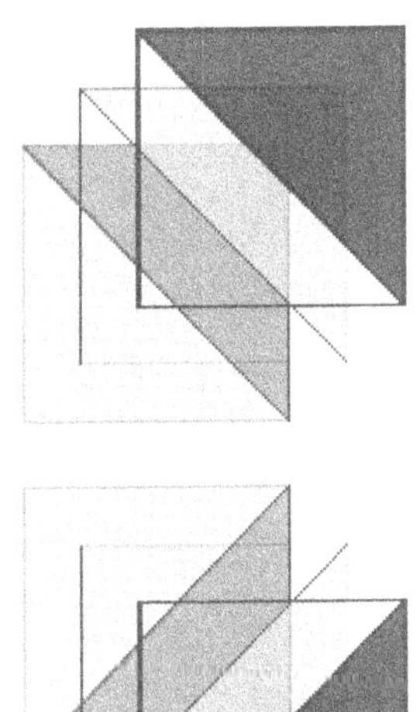

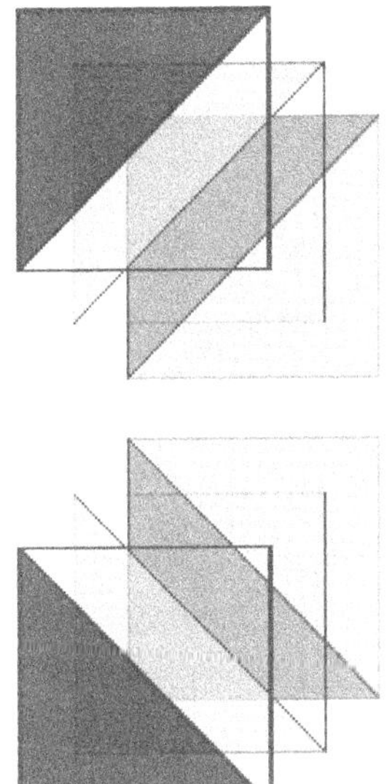

freedom

we are told
we have
a free country
yet our choices
are few
it's mostly
either red
or blue
we can go
here
but not there
say what we like
as long as
it's not that
we have choices
but not really
for some
things come
quite easy
for others
clearly
no matter
how hard
they work
it's a struggle
for freedom
it seems
you have to be very rich
or box clever
and even then
it's more likely
with the first one
not the other
freedom
not so pure

or true
and for most
it's a ruse

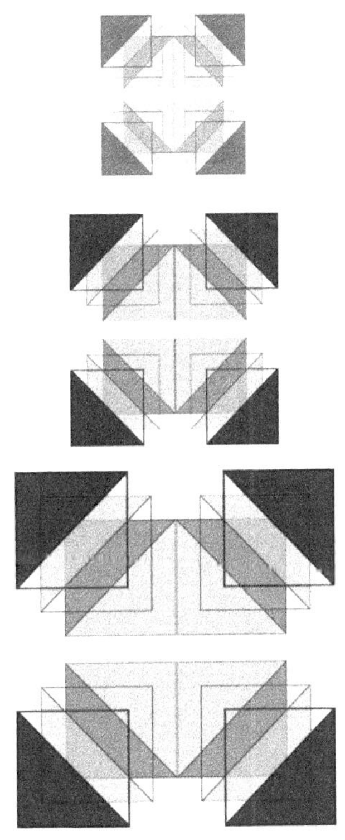

we are worried
about being
taken over by
machines
what if
the machine
shows us
more empathy
than
a human being?
what if
on average
all machines
are less mean
more polite
and make
all of us
seen?

numbers
you say they
don't lie
but do they
really
tell you
the truth?
do we measure
value
only by
popularity
and
revenue?

adrenalin
not fight
or flight
just other things
the do do
things
the can't stop
got to be
somewhere
clock
ticking
if i sleep
later
i win

nothing
i clicked
the thing
i always click
and today
or at least
right now
nothing
i thought
i ought
to ask someone
i looked to see how
but aught works
where i can find out
i'm sure
i wrote it all down
but i can't find that
piece of paper
as long as the lights too
don't go out
i will hopefully find it
later

the conversation
it's a journey
every time
sometimes
it's a pleasure
boat ride
but then
it can be
a walk
while tired
lots of stumbling
a conversation
though
even when it's
the last thing
for your current mood
or the one that's food
for your thinking
or just
a conversation
about nothing
it
i think
is always
worth having

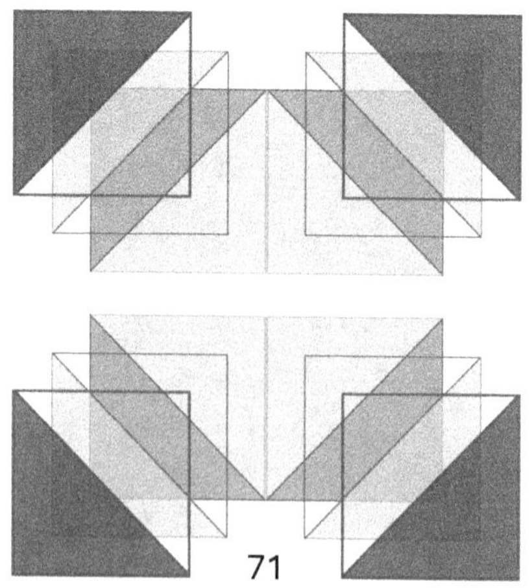

today
i did something
good
by good i mean
i did it well
for it being good
it depends
on how
it's seen
or understood
i may have spent
all passed times
doing that
very same thing
badly
but you didn't
find me here
shouting it out
gladly
if you had
maybe
it would be
quite different
how you
in your mind
find me

i would

if i knew
i'd be ok
but there are
powerful folk
who would
take note
of every word
and use them
not necessarily
or just
against me
but those
who are close
too
so i can't
just speak out
and say
i don't like the way
they play

it's true

i knew
but i went ahead
so did you
we both knew
i mean
i told you
you chose not to listen
though you definitely
heard me
and i heard you
i made the sandwiches
one with marmite spread
the other the same
just mixed in
peanut butter
but i had no idea
you disliked brown bread
at least
you brought the fruit
instead of one apple
have mine
too

i am
prejudice
seeking
a fault
made of a toxin
a spike
in my thoughts
i was not born to do this
this is something
brought by a pain
or something taught
like all
i was surely
born to love?

i know
songwriters
who've written
10 songs
and shared every one
others
i know
have written
100s
and not a single
one
so i beg
please
don't be too critical
of the brave
and too
those who are not
for some of us
[it] is hard enough
just
waking up

statements
of fact
well can they all
be true?
we use them
to expose
as we disclose
what we perceive
to be true
we saw them
from a certain angle
and in a type of light
so we are witness
but that person
stood
over there
they saw it too
their angle
in both sight
and thought
as is the light
in and from their court
different to ours
and so
it seems
their truth

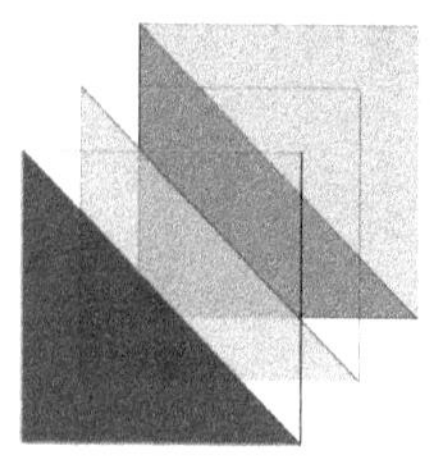

i look
at what i have
recently done
and i find it
to me
uninspired
i see
read
and hear
earlier stuff
it seems
less weary
a lot less forced
or tired
i look
back
just few days
not on today's
evidence
but that was me
it transpires!

only

1 week left
as it was last
to get the best
we can offer
and then
the day after
we will
still
let you have it
because we are so cool
the same
though the deadline
did pass
but hurry
it'll be another week
till we continue
this farse

we talk
the world
continues to turn
our views
well churned
grace
or pollute
the air space
depending
on your view
it's times we
look forward to
as the tea shops
and coffee shops
of the world
to seeing us
do too

just one more
slice he said
i'm sure
it'll be fine
it's not like
another cup of coffee
or glass of wine
how could it be
so bad?
i mean it's tasty
it makes him happy
well for a minute
then he says it again
till it's all finished
i'll
erm
i mean he'll
just say it had gone bad
when the kids ask
what happened to
the rest of it?

a routine
but
flexibility
is key
yes
i need to eat
and ideally
3 times
a mini feast
2 either side
of a long sleep
but i won't
pin my life
to that mast
we are not clocks
and i will not
be checked
or will i clock in
it shouldn't be
all a hard graft
a routine
but the boundaries
wider
and more space
between
the things we need to do
more moments
to breathe
and do the things
that keep us
keen

fast
as it all
comes
as the
mornings do
at you
need
to catch
at least
a few
but i'm
in no hurry
not really
they'll come round
again
next time
hopefully
more slowly
and
i've got one hand
holding toast
the other
clutching
my coffee
and i'm not
letting go
not for them
not for you

a quirk

a nervous laugh
some call them tics
some gaffs
no different
to an erm
a like
y'know
others get irritable
annoyed
wear their thoughts
on the outside
or on the inside and
often
overboil
our disorder
keeps
our inner order
as much as it tries
and it can
it's just how
we flow
and it's how we
remember
and understand
the folk
we know

i am

art
do not
define me
i will drive you
to all sorts
love
displeasure
and all
variety
of insanity
a soul bared
and mostly
ignored
often leading
to discord
even infamy
but when
fame finds
me
all that was
found
with words
unkind
suddenly
pestered
hounded
and suffocated
adoringly
as
my soul
is
sold
for
money

sorry
please
indulge me
my words
are rarely
about me
but today
i am weary
mainly of
being measured
by a tool
but it was like
measuring a litre
of water
with a slide rule
i work on many planes
just right now
i am writing a song
as i am a poem
and not either related
i could be
mean into a mean
using algebraic ways
whilst cooking up a notion
and drawing souffles
you could say a jack
of many trades
yet master to some
on all planes
if not master
to the master
of each
but enough to please
and i do
what works for
and pleases me

and please
and so sorry
don't measure me
with tools
not fit
or against
mediocrity

lip service
it's not lip balm
used to coerce
and charm
sometimes
to keep
detractors
calm
the truth is
it's a lie
i won't lie
it's lipstick
as the americans
say it
on a swine
in any other guise

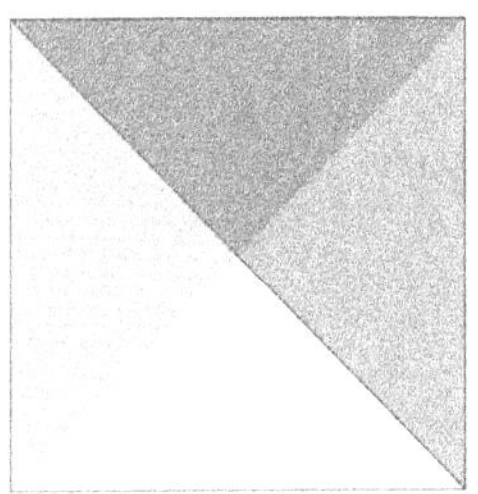

taste
i like red
you like orange
a tomato
and olives
or salad
with lettuce
not cabbage
some
like onions
raw
like others
do apples
and those who
eat marmite
by the spoon
now just because
they're not quite
like you
or seemingly
to you
not quite there
does it make them
or to them
you
loons?

fun
why not?
under the moon
whatever we do
whatever is going on
sometimes
even
in the very worst
of them
fun
helps us
carry on
so whatever it is
and when
under the sun
why not?

someone said
something
that was wrong
well i believed
not on a podium
or a popular song
just into a void
in a public house
or was it
the internet?
a void
just the same
yet by my voicing
disagreement
the world blew up
into pitchfork battle
and war song

a battle
it suggests
somebody loses
and somebody wins
though some
seem essential
how can we bring
a fight
where nobody loses
and everybody wins?
now
i think
that would be
a special
battle

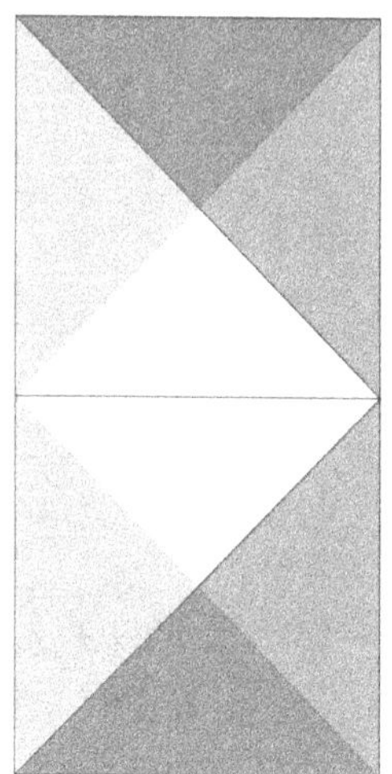

we
in words
honour the brave
we rave
we rave
they do
and say
the things
we pretend
we would
when
we rage
we rage
and when
their life
is made undone
we still
do nothing
more
than in words
for their deeds
rave
and
continue
again
in words
to rage

we let them
even though
we know
who
and how
they are
we know
how
it's going
to play
yet we say
surely
it cannot be
no one can be
and it plays
exactly that way
and we say
we knew
how it would be
yet
it's we
we let them

people
it's the making
of them
the good spaces
and the bad
yet we seek solace
in empty ones
away from them all
and yet again
without other folk
it's not so easy
to be rid of
what makes us sad
our fear of strangers
a belief
not always unfounded
that they
may
do us harm
if only that thought
were wiped empty
we would know
in truth
we and them
could make
each other
glad

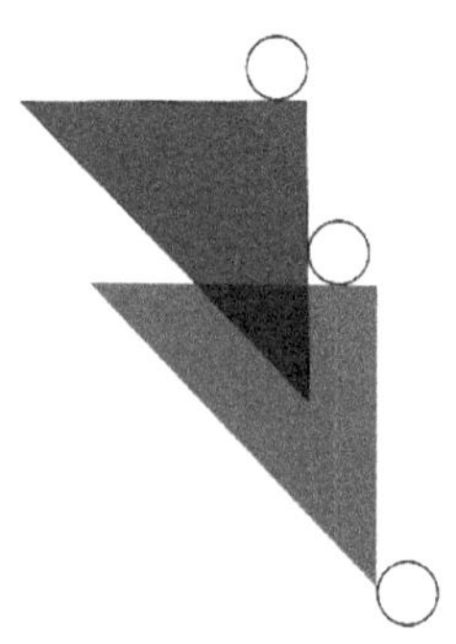

a heart shaped
balloon
in the crescent
of the moon
is the only
we[e] moment
we stopped
as the day
ran away

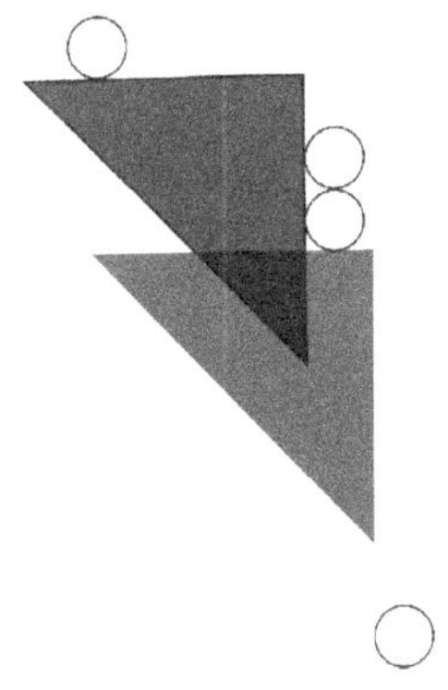

sound
brings me round
in rhythm
food
for another

parallel

we draw them
we shout
sometimes
it's not quite
but we draw them
to fell
sometimes
to swell
we draw them
rarely well

the poles
the helmet
the skies
time a lot
on my bum
metaphorically
on my knees
though the view
from the piste
is quite something
and the kids
are having
quite a lot
of fun

you're due
a poem
i know
but the day
it's not
a normal one
we
have been having
far too much fun

bonjour
i say
they say the same
then
how can i help?
i'm sure
unless
my french
has much improved
that was english
with which
they responded
was my
bonjour said
in an accent
that poor?
well they
were kind
and very friendly
which
for any ailing day
is the perfect
cure

the night

i am
not usually
much of a witness
i sleep more
than i often confess
it brings a brighter
brightness
to my days
though tonight
i have another
confession
there is
much to delight
even
in darkness
so stay up
sometimes
i must
and i will
if not too often
now i have found
a reason

it was fun
that thing we did
not sure
it was more
than that once
yet i
and the last time
we said anything
you
still remember it
despite
all the things
that passed
between
to me
that was
the best
game of
ping pong
there ever
was
or has since
been

why is it
we
rightly
spend
so much
money
[on]
saving a life
yet with
one bomb
bought
using
the very same
money
we kill
so
so
many?

a thousand
miles per second
we travel
on this vessel
yet
we are
mostly
still
and often
feel nil

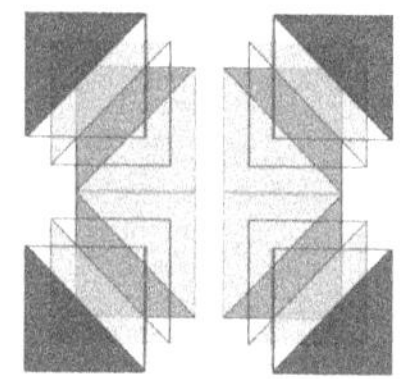

a failure
everyone is
particularly
the very best
and more so
the ones
with the most
success
i wonder
if those
who shout
at you
with bitterness
and mock
and boo
are only upset
because they
can't take a ride
on what they can't
and what you
far better than they
do
do?

a list
you've written
one
actually a few
because
someone said
you need to
but life
it doesn't like it
it looks
and looks again
often
at this list
and all it does
is build up
anxious mist

indeed

i wonder
if we
i mean generically
we woke up
and didn't see
an enemy
just everybody
as part of the team
cogs in our own machine
some worn
some broken
some not
but without each other
we are naught

*in response to someone else's poem about
fairness in life generally*

the willingness to think
beyond and then do
to look at something
and think
yes that word again
how it might be different
or better or renewed
to spark a thought from the arbitrary
and turn it into something
interesting
at least
interesting to you
everyone can do that
just some for some reason
refuse

to the perennial question of talent or hard work
asked by another writer on @threads

the morning
it's good
i've had some food
and a hot drink
with milk
and then calm
after the rush
to catch a train
or the school bus
to work
to study
or do
to enjoy the norm
how lucky we are
those
of my ilk

if life were
a thick
thick book
full of stuff
not a guide
just substance
and fluff
we work one
enjoy the other
if life were
how do we know
which pages
to read
or where
to look?

take a bow
you made it
some make out
it's the easiest thing
but [they] aren't you
their time
was back then
when they
made sense
of everything
yours
is now

our time
it's finite
well at least
i think
so as not
to chance it
i'd like to make
the best
of every bit

the edit
i let
someone else look
they see
the things we don't
i wonder
if it's things we won't
we are our own
zealots
but what if
someone
is one too?
how do i
separate
their
and my beliefs
from
truth?
facts are easy
but it seems
when each someone speaks
each fact
from each and every
one of them
has many truths
no wonder
we get confused

what is it
to get to the crest?
is it a bag full
of trophies
awards?
it often drags
a bag full
with it
of others'
expectations
and a lot
of stress
sometimes
loneliness
who defines
what is best?
what's best
for you
not so others
can take a ride
on your news
the crest
selfish
or selfless
is surely
happiness?

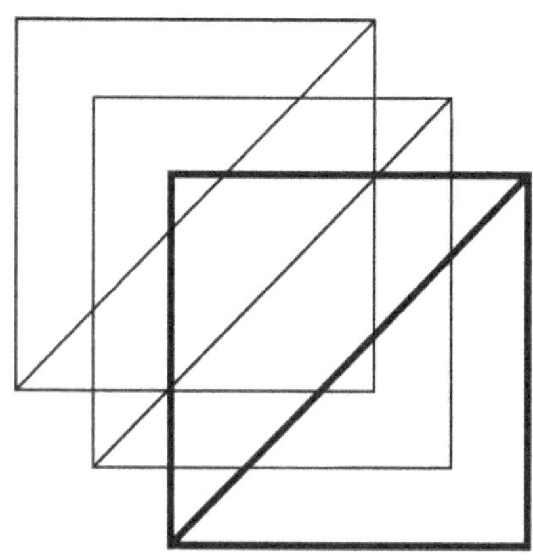

doing the thing
the one i should
even if
no one else would
it's definitely
the right thing
to do
the consequence
of not
just won't do
things will fester
this indecision
makes no one
better
so i'll take
the last slice
of cake

i'm not ready
i don't know why
i started this
today
i'm not ready
for anything
i haven't finished
yesterday yet
i was too tired
so i went to bed
i've started this now
so i'll finish that
at some point
today
it has to be
but i don't know how
i'm not ready
i said

we repeat
when we sit down
again
with friends
or even those
you just met
once
and now again
we repeat
the stories
we have often told
so when you grow old
and people say
you repeat
the same thing
again
and again
tell them
to stop saying that
again
and again
and don't forget
to repeat that
often
when ever
and when

i have my routine
well i say that
i prefer not
yes i go to sleep
roughly
the same time
as i do eat
i often have coffee
not long after my first tea
but rigid it's not
we are smart
and complex enough
to meander
the incoming
random
flying pots
yes there are set things
with set times
like when to pick up the kids
and when to drink wine
ok maybe not that
but yes there is all that stuff
but[so?] why take away
the freedoms we've got?
we are clever enough
to negotiate
each and every
pot

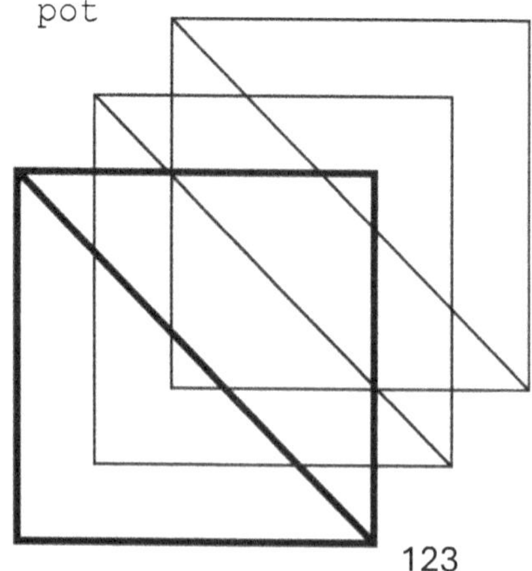

i'm going
to do that next
i said to myself
last time
and this time
but this time
i'm going
to get that done
just after
i've done this thing
for kid no.2
and then help
and make food
with kid no.1
and then i'll
perhaps rest
take a minute
to myself
then
then
then
before i know
the day is
yet again
before
i can do that thing
done

we could
be on a train
on a long journey
sit in our seat
and never get off
till we reach
the final stop
or we could
be on a bus
that stops everywhere
change seats at every stop
sometimes get off
and stay
and catch it again
tomorrow
or next week
or never again
why not?

set aside
our differences
we say
we are the same
but that's
too easy to claim
difference
is different
from
a different perspective
change the light
and what we see
can be
a sea change
so in my view
embrace that
we share
but what that is
is different
points of view

a new
dawn
a new age
we draw a line
we turn a page
the billboards
the headline news
and the choristers
from their pews
we bought the cards
the food
and the boose
then
woke up the
next morning
to the same
old you

it's just

another distraction
some call it bait
it plays
on our
propensity
to rage
and move it along
as they
turn the page

we live
for love
for our children
for music
our craft
that train set in the attic
the engine in the garage
half built
quilting that quilt
if we are lucky
that is
that we have time
and money for it
yet no matter
what the struggle
it is the poetry
that keeps us
or at least tries
from feeling solitary
at [the] worst and best
of it

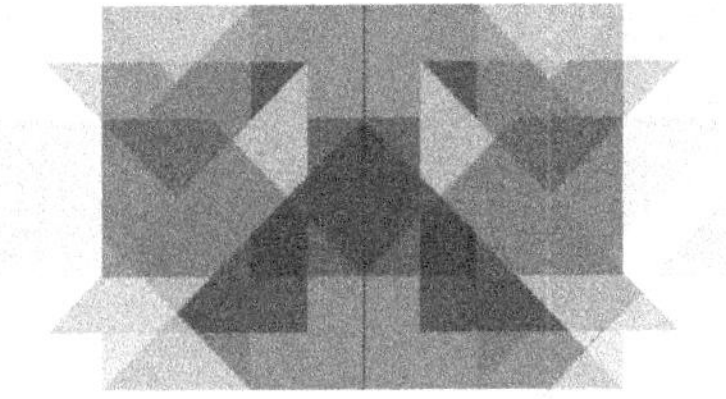

a machine

sent me a message
asked me a thing
then another thing
this wasn't a scam thing
but a proper thing
something
that could be
an important thing
something
i'd have expected
in times past
and less testing
a person
with knowhow
the sort
that universities
and the like
dish out
would be answering
but instead
now
i am told
how i am
and what to do
by
not a human being
but
a machine

tie them up
in knots
with stuff
that doesn't
really mean
that much
but just enough
to distract them
from the stuff
you want to do
that would
if they really
understood
mean lots
it in turn
and they never
learn
makes you
pots and pots
then
you can
distract them
again
with news
so they buy
the pots
off you

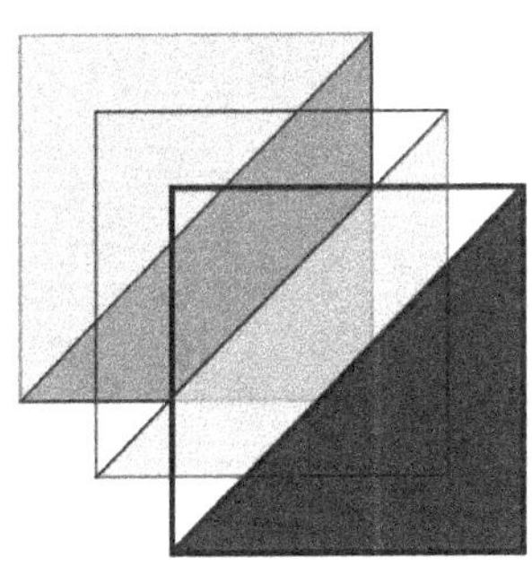

i'll use words
again
as i have
used before
maybe by this
my limitations
are let loose
for all to see
free
and
a vulnerability
i'll use words
and again
i've used them here
already
and when
we meet again
we'll both
repeat
a thought
or a story
we told
already
that word again
two or three
times at least

i have to decide
which way
to be
today
do i drive
or do i sit
on the passenger side?
it can't be
always me
at the wheel
sometimes
and times
more than mine
it's not just
their turn
but better
that they guide
through
and into
the difficult turns
sometimes
it's better
i don't decide

didn't stop much
not for that much
more than
a few minutes
doing this
seeing that
conversation
hopping
one serious
about money
next one
more casual
funny
yes
that's all
i could find
to rhyme
with money
a coffee here
an offer of cake
there
and i had tea
with it
that was to chime
with minute
and yes
i'll need to unwind
having had
so much caffeine
and i'm not
no
actually
i think i am
finished

i miss you
you crispy chew
it's been a few days
since i had you
a pack of 8
is far too few
next time i shop
i'll buy 2

in response to a poetry prompt, i miss you, on threads.